Truth in **PRIVATE** Lending

Truth in
PRIVATE
Lending

Real Estate Investors Guide to
Keeping Scammers Away From Your Money

RANDY P. HINKLE

New York

Truth in **PRIVATE** Lending
Real Estate Investors Guide to Keeping
Scammers Away From Your Money

Published in New York, New York, by Morgan James Publishing. Morgan James and The Entrepreneurial Publisher are trademarks of Morgan James, LLC.
www.MorganJamesPublishing.com

The Morgan James Speakers Group can bring authors to your live event. For more information or to book an event visit The Morgan James Speakers Group at www.TheMorganJamesSpeakersGroup.com.

Shelfie

A **free** eBook edition is available
with the purchase of this print book.

CLEARLY PRINT YOUR NAME ABOVE IN UPPER CASE

Instructions to claim your free eBook edition:
1. Download the Shelfie app for Android or iOS
2. Write your name in **UPPER CASE** above
3. Use the Shelfie app to submit a photo
4. Download your eBook to any device

ISBN 978-1-63047-801-8 paperback
ISBN 978-1-63047-803-2 eBook
ISBN 978-1-63047-802-5 hardcover
Library of Congress Control Number:
2015915277

Cover Design by:
Chris Treccani
www.3dogdesign.net

Interior Design by:
Bonnie Bushman
The Whole Caboodle Graphic Design

In an effort to support local communities and raise awareness and funds, Morgan James Publishing donates a percentage of all book sales for the life of each book to Habitat for Humanity Peninsula and Greater Williamsburg

Get involved today, visit
www.MorganJamesBuilds.com

Habitat
for Humanity®
Peninsula and
Greater Williamsburg
Building Partner

TABLE OF CONTENTS

PREFACE

As an investor myself, I felt an enormous need to write this book. Even with as much hands-on experience as I have had, I know how hard it is to see the truth or read between the lines. My goal in writing this book is to educate and inform investors on how to decide if their lender is a legitimate source of funding, or a scam. In the following chapters I will explain what the warning signs are in different types of scams and fraudulent activities. I will explain why it is important to handle things with patience, and leave emotional factors out of the decision process about your lender. In this book you will find detailed accounts of personal experiences I have had with a wide variety of fraudulent private lenders. Some scammers I can detect immediately upon reading their first e-mail. Others are so sophisticated, they are virtually impossible to figure out and avoid, without some good guidelines to follow.

This book is focused on real events and circumstances related to real estate investing. I will not go in to detail on other unrelated types of scams, but I will give you some tips on sound real estate investing practices. I am trying to get you inside the con-artist's mind. If you can see your deal as they do, you will be better prepared to protect yourself, your money, and your valuable time. We need to watch out for these types of people in our everyday life and in our business life. I also will discuss your personal safety when traveling and meeting with private lenders, and identity theft and how it can occur.

I really hate to sound so negative, but the facts are that 90 to 99 percent of the lending sources you come into contact with in private lending are scams. Unfortunately, this makes locating and closing the funding extremely difficult. So, I am providing a few chapters to describe in detail what is required to get funded, and how to safely work through the application and underwriting procedures. My hope is that with this book, you will become more aware of the many types of scams that exist, and will be able to successfully avoid them to find the funding you need to achieve your goals.

I would like all readers to know that 20 percent of the net proceeds of this book will donated to the Stoney

Creek Outreach, Inc., a 501(c)(3) non-profit that I have been involved with, to help it continue its amazing work helping under-privileged youth.

Chapter One
WHY WE NEED FUNDING

All investors need funding to make purchases. Here is our biggest problem. We know there is a ton of money potentially available for us to borrow to make us and the private lender happy. This gives us a false sense of hope though, because even though the money is real, we do not have the patience and know-how to get to those private lenders in the correct fashion. These lenders will typically not loan to us unless we have a direct connection to them, to make them feel confident in us as a borrower. We know that we are honest, and believe this should be a simple deal. Sometimes we even think we are doing them a favor. When we can't find what we need, we go blindly hunting online for a lender, instead of looking for what we really need to get this done—the direct contact.

This is where the problem starts. Impatience that leads to looking in the wrong place for the wrong thing, never finding the contacts that will connect you with a real lender. I can give you huge list of great buys I had on contract or a Letter of Intent(LOI) that would have made me a millionaire several times over—if the lenders that had promised the funding had closed the deal. We all know this process can be an emotional roller coaster. I am just like you and I want my deals to work! I have the emotional highs and then the depressing lows when things fall apart. I get sick when an investor contacts me about being scammed, knowing that each time it happens, it puts distance between them and real success. Consider the following investor's scenario:

You think you have a legitimate private lender and they guarantee you they will deliver your loan after you pay an origination fee of $5,000. You pay that, but then they come back and approve your loan, but tell you that you will have to pay a transfer fee of $2,000. In the end they back out and do not close. At this point you have lost $7,000 of your down payment money, and this makes you even more desperate for a deal to close. A few months later you still have not had any success. One day while you're in this desperate state, a nice professional-speaking lender calls and asks you if you have a deal they can fund. Of course, being a real estate investor, you always keep one in your back pocket.

We go down the same path of filling out the lender's application, sending all of our personal data, and then suddenly they turn your loan down. Three months later you find out they have used your identity to obtain a credit card and used $5,000 in credit, which you have to pay. Now you are $12,000 in the hole, and very desperate, because you have almost exhausted half the funds you had originally. A few months later you find a great deal, you think you have a real lender that has everything in order and nothing unusual. You pay $2,500 for the appraisal and their origination fee of $3,000. You wait and let other deals pass by since you are sure this deal is going to work. Then the lender calls you back and tells you the appraisal has come back short by $100,000! The deal is over because you do not have the $100,000. This deal is another $5,500 loss.

All these losses from bad decisions add up to $17,500. Now I want you to think about how much time has elapsed, six to twelve months! If you had used the $17,500 as a down payment on a property that was affordable based on that down payment, you could have purchased an $87,500 property with a 20% down payment. If you made a really good buy you would sell the property at around $110,000 net. This investment would have cleared you $22,500, plus you have your $17,500 you put down. Now you have $40,000 to buy a $200,000 property. You sell it for $260,000 or 30% gain, which is $60,000 plus you have the $40,000 you started with, and now you have $100,000, and still have not used up half the time you wasted in the original scam lender scenario above.

When looking for funding, we should always consider our personal and local bankers first. They will always have the best deal for us if we can get qualified for the needed amount. This is an issue that has changed dramatically, as some public lending institutions are scared to death of investors like us because of bad past experiences. Not all of those experiences were from bad investor decisions, some were from their own overly aggressive bankers—which is what we like! Aggressive lending may be a thing of the past for some time, but they will need business eventually, and they will begin to forget those bad loans. At that point they will start easing the criteria and qualification process, and the loan amount, or Loan to Value (LTV), will start to gradually increase again.

Lets assume you cannot get qualified for a loan at your local bank. You still have numerous options depending on your financial situation, and the property.

There are private lenders, capital raises, crowd funding, institutional money, international investors, family, friends, and the Small Business Administration. These are some of the major avenues we can go down to find funding for our deal.

Private lenders are typically people with their own cash they are lending. This can be a group, and you typically are not speaking with the person that has the money, but with a broker. Another way to describe them is to say they are lenders without a store front, office, company name, etc. Capital raises are when you actually find investors yourself or have someone find them and you have a goal of some specified amount. You keep contacting cash investors until you reach your goal. Typically these investors want a return on their money invested and an equity portion of your investment or acquisition. Crowd funding is very similar to capital raises but there are much smaller amounts received from many more smaller investors to get to the funding needed. Institutional investors are basically hedge funds. International investors could be any of these categories, but located outside the United States. Of course, family and friends are self-explanatory.

First let's consider the deal. What is it? Do we have a contract? Is it one property or a group? Do we have the property identified? What is the loan amount needed? What is the as-is and as repaired value (ARV)? What is our credit score? Does the property produce income? Is it in need of major repairs? If so do we have that experience? Two major factors to consider: How much experience in the industry related to our loan do we have? How much money do we have of our own, our skin in the game, to use as a down payment?

Before I go down the road of making private lenders look bad, let me first apologize to the good ones. This is not intended to bash the entire industry. True legitimate lenders lose their money and time just as often as the borrowers. There are many unscrupulous borrowers who lie on their applications, fraudulently furnish documentation, and back out of closing when the loan is ready. One indicator that you are dealing with a legitimate lender is that if you mention escrow for fees, they do not run. They understand it is a normal business practice. It's important as a private investor to realize how the bad and good see this so differently.

I will discuss each of our deal questions above one by one.

First, what kind of deal are you trying to fund? I read a document from a reputable private lender that had an example of two borrowers with different types of properties. One was an income generating property and the other was a faith-based property. The lender used the property type as the deciding factor. They approved the loan on the income producing property, and declined the faith-based building, because it is hard to market. This decision is a no-brainer for me, as I work as an appraiser. But, for some investors they do not see it from the lender's perspective. This can result in time and money wasted. Once I did have a faith-based distressed property that I got approved with a good private lender, but the deal had a good bit of expensive vacant commercial property on the road frontage. It did require some skin in the game on my part as well. We need to be aware of how the lender we are dealing with feels about our property type. We need to search for lenders who are interested in our property type before we engage them. Another important thought, private lenders always make decisions based on the possibility of getting the property back. So good locations are always preferred. We all know how important location is in real estate. If you have not heard this statement, get a real estate book and study location, it is truly the number one factor to consider in buying.

Lenders will typically not give you the time of day if you do not have the property under contract or you have a secure *Letter of Intent (LOI)*. They are not interested in wasting their valuable time. If you do not have a contract or LOI, they have no guarantee that you can buy the property and that the price is set, which has a direct effect on loan amount. Contracts tell the lender many important things. It gives them the price, the legal description, and the type of transfer (fee simple, leasehold, or fee estate). Most lenders only deal in fee simple, meaning you buy the land, the buildings, and all rights except subsurface rights. It tells them the time window they have to close their loan with you. Most of the time it tells how much money you have to put down, what is required of you to pay at closing, and what the seller is required to pay. A contract also let's the lender know if you have left out any important elements like inspections, repairs, or taxes and other prepaids.

If the deal is a single property it is the simplest form of transaction for financing in most instances. That being said, I will tell you that it is sometimes easier to get bigger deals done than smaller ones. The lender may prefer having less deals that are larger, rather than the same dollar amount in multiple, smaller loans. It is less work, and the tenants are typical closer to credit tenants. A credit tenant is a company that has received a good rating based on their financial strength from one of the major rating companies.

I prefer to buy in larger numbers which gives me a less risky portfolio. It lets you cost-average your occupancies and tenants over the entire portfolio instead of having so much risk in only a few tenants. If a tenant bankrupts, the smaller portfolio is hurt badly, but for the larger it is just a small bump in the road.

Have you actually picked out the property you want to buy? There are some very important factors in having your property picked out before going after funding. Without the specific property and the price, you have no idea what to put on an application as a requested loan amount. You need to know this as much as the lender. You can only make an educated decision on what to pay if you have two things, a contract price and terms of your loan. This is why cash flow analysis based on a specific price is so important. Second, If you do not have a specific property tied up in the form of a letter of intent or contract then the lender typically will not proceed with underwriting your request. They know some other party could buy that property if you do not have it secured properly, and all the work they had done would be wasted with no possibility of making a fee off your loan.

Most find the property first, but I like to have cash to buy before I go looking. Cash in hand gives you much greater negotiating power. I estimate that on average I can get about 20% off the price with cash compared to financing. If it is a distressed property, lenders really want to, and at times have to, get these properties off their books. When you have the cash they know you can close, and it takes out many of the contingencies in contract.

Without properties identified, you had better have a great business plan, a proven track record, and loads of experience.

Once you have the contract or LOI, you have established a purchase price. So, now we as investors want the highest loan-to-value or loan to purchase price (two different things) we can possibly obtain. The higher we get the less cash we have to use for each deal, and the more deals we can do. If you are like me it is all about numbers. You want to make as much as you can get. I am assuming you have enough experience to buy the right deals, at the right price, and in the right location. In bigger deals it is much easier to get a higher LTV than with smaller ones. Lenders get more aggressive because they will fight for the larger deals that are above $1 million. In most cases the lenders require a 65% LTV. Here are two scenarios: The first is a straight purchase with no rehab. At this point the lender typically uses the sale price or appraised value as the value to determine the LTV or loan amount. On the second, you have to do some rehab work. In this case they use the *As Repaired Value (ARV)* to determine how much they will loan. Typically you will not get 100% funding. We all wish for 100% funding, but it is rare. It takes a lot of closed contacts. Just expect a 20% down payment. I think you will have to work at that to get it, but an 80% LTV is in the realm of possibilities.

How is your credit? If you have an LLC (Limited Liability Corporation) many lenders will not even pull your credit, depending on all other factors being considered. But most want to see that you care about paying your bills on time. In most cases the magic credit score range is 650-700 to get approved. Some factors that may help if your credit is not in range are: if the property is decent, if the price is really good, or if they would have bought it on the open market. That last statement is very important! If the private lender does not think the deal is good, they will not make the loan unless the amount of the loan or LTV is very low, like 50% or lower, based on a conservative appraisal.

This is another complaint I have, being an appraiser for thirty years I understand the thought process of the purchase price establishing the value. Just as a warning, when you buy really low some appraisals do not reflect the true market value, let me explain further. It is true that when your purchase closes it establishes value for future sales. But, the appraiser has to list that sale as a distressed sale if it is or why it sold below normal market value. That tells me without a doubt, that if I buy a property worth $1 million and it is nice with a **NNN lease(triple net lease, which means no landlord responsibilities) and NOI (Net Operating Income)** of $200,000 then the value is closer to $2 million. But, I have had deals just like that and the appraisal comes back in at $900,000 or $1.03 million, which is not right in my opinion. You should not be penalized for being smart.

Does the property you have under contract produce income? If not, good luck! There are some instances where you need to have a tenant sign a lease before closing, but that is still income producing at that point. If the income is really high based on the purchase price *Cap Rate (Net Income/Purchase), at 10% or above, that is a plus for lenders. A 10% return on the purchase price is great, and the actual rate of return on their money is much higher. This is called cash-on-cash Return on Investment (ROI). The cash-on-cash return equals the amount invested in cash divided by the annual pre-tax cash flow. The buyer puts down 20% to buy the deal, and finances the rest. You then take the financing cost (an expense item) out of the net operating income, and what is left you take the down payment amount* and divide by the net of debt service net income. This is a very important factor in lending or investing: buy what has income. If not, you need to do a lot of homework to prove you can get the property rented to 80% to 90% occupancy in 12 months, and have the cash reserves to get to that point. Some lenders will loan reserve funds for that 12 month period so you do not get in trouble. Always calculate and understand the *lenders Return on Investment (ROI). The*

ROI equals the gross profit minus expenses (including the original investment), divided by the expenses. This is the return based on the total cost as a percentage of its income.

Does your purchase need repairs? This can be an important factor if you have limited money on hand. If it needs major work and you have to use outside sources for the repairs, get good estimates for those costs before engaging the lender, this shows you know what you are doing. If a property needs major repairs I would recommend that anyone without a ton of experience to stay away from those type deals. If you have the experience to do repairs correctly yourself, this may give you an option that will help close the deal. Get a bid from a very good contractor, and give that bid to the lender for the estimate of repairs. Then do the work yourself for less. They appreciate those who have the ability to save money and do the repairs themselves, it makes their loan less risky, because you are saving money and taking out a loan with a lower LTV. Don't underestimate your repair costs! This is where many novice investors get into trouble. They do not know how to correctly cushion the cost of repairs. If you unrealistically estimate repair costs you are left with less funds than are needed to get the property back to income producing levels, and you have no income to pay debt service. It leaves a bad taste in the lender's mouth when you come back for more funds for repairs, which they may decide not to approve.

Lenders will evaluate your experience. There are many questions about you that a lender will use to determine if you are a good borrower. Some questions are: How many years in the industry do you have? Do you know if you are paying too much or getting a deal? Do you know how to look for repairs and can you be trusted to get real and fair estimate? Can you negotiate well from the experience of many closed deals before? Can you write a contract, or do you have someone in place to write it? Can you manage the property after closing? Do you have management lined up and have that cost included in projected budget? Can you market the deal if you want to resell it? Positive answers to these questions give the lender peace of mind. If there are areas that you are inexperienced in, have an experienced professional help and give the lender their credentials. If you can provide this experience yourself or show that you have other experienced people involved, you will stand out from other potential borrowers to your private lender.

Last and most important is how much skin in the game you can produce. If you have little experience, then you will need more personal commitment. I would recommend having a 35% down payment ready, at minimum. Remember, lenders lend when they feel good about getting paid back. If the deal has complications such as repairs, then have a plan for those complications before engaging the lender. As we discussed earlier, if you are lucky and you have experience, then 10% down is realistic and a great deal.

THE BASIC LIST OF REAL ESTATE INVESTING

1. Identify what type of property you can afford and manage.

2. Identify what is needed for funding and obtain three to five lenders that fit your property type and situation, and do your due diligence. Get pre-qualified.

3. Take your criteria for your perfect property and write it down. Specifically list what characteristics your property has to have to be worthwhile.

4. Identify on paper what your sources are for finding this property.

5. Use that list to identify potential properties to purchase.

6. Start the negotiation process on the top property on your list. If your negotiations are not successful, go back to number two on the list.

7. Get a signed Letter of Intent to purchase from the seller. List each item just like the contract will have and make sure you have the proper items, please be sure to have a due diligence period. It

is a common practice in commercial properties. The length of this period is yours to choose, but is typically directly related to the complexity of the property. This due diligence period gives you what I call, a free look period.

8. After getting the LOI signed, give it to the top verified lender on your list with a request for funding. Have an executive summary prepared so the lender knows the who, what, where and when of your deal. Get the lender to give you an LOI on the funding.

9. Get a full legal contract on the property, be careful and have a professional write this contract. It can be you if you're qualified, or a Realtor or attorney. Make sure everything needed is listed, this is not rocket science but very important. Remember this is a legal agreement. Hand this contract over to the lender, it is their road map in the transaction.

10. If the funding is moving along in a positive manner, prepare to get your due diligence completed. At this point you cannot walk away from it without an extraordinary circumstance known by the Realtor or seller that they did not disclose.

11. Get your funding completed and close!

Chapter Two
THE CATEGORIES OF RISK

H ere are the most common categories of risk:

Fraud. They will have a high fee that you can't afford, so they have an "investor" pay it for you. They wire funds to you that are either stolen, counterfeit, or from some other source that will not clear in a few days. Then they have you wire those funds to an account that has nothing to do with your loan. It will have a made up purpose, either an insurance premium to cover the loan as collateral, or a fee to transfer. Once you send it out you find out the funds are not good, and now you are liable for the funds you sent. Unfortunately the lender is gone.

Employment fraud. A large company will send you an e-mail asking you to work for them. Usually something simple with very little effort to make a good bit of money. It sounds like a great deal that would give you some income while you are working on the real estate that you love. They send you what seems to be a real contract. Your "job" will involve transferring money to different accounts for what appears to be a legitimate reason. These wire transfers will come from some account with counterfeit funds and you will send them on to another account. You may end up liable for any funds used after being in your account for multiple days.

Fee Scams. It's a bait and switch. The lender gets you to pay a very small fee, then asks for more and more. They never intend to actually fund you.

Identity Theft. We all know most lenders have to have a good bit of our personal information to approve us for funding. When we do this we open the door for nightmares. Potentially scammers can take your credit information to get credit cards which they will max out. Unfortunately you may not find out for months, and could be held liable.

Circumventing. This is where someone uses your information and goes behind you and buys a property you are trying to buy. If you are ever concerned about this, get a non-circumvent agreement before sending details to a lender about your great deal you are about to buy. It can be purchased by the unethical lender behind your back.

There are many different scenarios for each of these categories. We will discuss actual experiences I have had that can give you the insight to see what is going on before you get into trouble. Remember, lenders struggle with scams as well. As reputable lenders, they also have issues from their side from unethical borrowers. Borrowers will use a low appraisal, which the lender has nothing to do with, to file a lawsuit against them. Borrowers will lie about things to try to get qualified. They are wasting the lenders valuable time and their own. Borrowers can used stolen identities, fictitious properties and so forth to try to scam the lender, especially if they are direct private lenders that may not even ask for an appraisal. As you read about the following scams, remember that reputable lenders have just as hard a time finding reputable and ethical borrowers.

Chapter Three

HOW TO SEE THROUGH
THE DECEPTION

We have discussed controlling our emotions earlier, and this is a major concern—even for me! You must get control of your thoughts and stay focused on what is real. Scam artists are good, they evolve into what they need to be to think ahead of you. Unfortunately for us they can seem very real. So I am telling you now that by the time this book is printed and you are reading it, the scammers will have found hundreds of new ways to make us feel better about their scam, and convince us it is just a really great deal. They will play to your personality. They will use social media sites and learn all they can about you. For example, if they find you are deeply devoted to a religion, then they will become devoted to that religion, and use that to gain your trust. That one really bites me! It just shows how devious these people really are.

One of the most important things I can teach you is not to let them push you with time frames. This is a big red flag. What banker is going to push you to send a fee? Get your wiring information? Set up a bank account with no funds for them to get the password and user id? Never! Think about it when they ask for something odd. Ask why! Always slow things down. This is important because it gives you time to do your due diligence while you are putting them on hold. If you are getting pressured, tell them you are about to leave on a trip for several days and you will revisit the funding when you return, then study them. To do this, you have to get as much information as you can. Get their name, address, website, phone number, a copy of their driver's license, a copy of their lending license—get as much information as possible. Verify their business license, check to see if the phone numbers match. Even if they do, stay cautious and do not believe anything without verification. Frequently they forward their phone numbers from a US location back to a foreign country. That can be traced, as can an IP address. Spend the money to check their information with a service like BeenVerified. It is worth $22.86 a month to have that service available.

Look closely at their initial email! Look at the spelling, grammar, and punctuation. Do you think a guy that is about to loan you $2 million can't spell? If they can't spell or write a sentence, do not play around with them, just do not answer their calls or e-mails ever again. Because of these people I do not answer my cell phone unless I know the caller. They can leave a message, and if it is important, they will. Check their e-mail address and IP address. If you feel you need to, they are probably scamming. But, even if you feel great about them, check both, then check their phone number. Ask for their office number, references, or even proof of funds. If these things are provided, do not take their word for it that they are real. Many times they have fake information ready to provide, they are that good.

Ask them how they got your information when they contacted you. I list my requests for funding on my favorite business social media sites, which opens the door to all sorts of scammers and is probably a mistake. I honestly do not have time to pick up the phone and call lenders and talk or fill out application after application. Ask where they are located and verify it. Do not let them give you an excuse. Another easy way to get a quick answer is type in their name or business name in an internet search engine and at the end simply add scam to the search. Many times this will give you an answer immediately. Sometimes there will be rebuttals showing, trust me, they write those themselves. Lots of times the names will be changed though so they are harder to track on those sites.

I will tell you now I have personally been involved in things that I cannot explain how or why they did it! Things so big and unsafe I should be kicked for even getting close to where I placed myself. What is worth putting your life (yes your life) or your family's safety at risk? This may seem far-fetched to some, but trust me it is a real concern. No deal or amount of money is worth putting yourself or family in any of those situations. The financial risk is of course the most common. If you keep funneling fees to these people, before you know it, you have spent tens of thousands of dollars of your hard earned money. You will hardly ever get any money back by filing lawsuits or threatening them. The truth is you will probably never find them. The search would likely cost more than what they took. And if you did find them, what then? We really want to get even, but it probably will not happen. We may feel like we want to hunt them down and do something stupid, yes I am one of those type guys, but in reality we would only be hurting ourselves.

SIGNS OF BEING SCAMMED

This list is my thoughts on what to look for, if you think you think you are being scammed.

1. If a lender contacts you and has no contact information in the initial e-mail.
2. If the grammar in an e-mail is poor.
3. If the lender gets pushy.
4. If the interest rate is quoted and is very low.
5. If you do not know how the lender got your information.
6. If there name is very common.
7. If there are twenty people on social media with that name.
8. If the application is in the email body (very common).
9. If they approve your funding in less than 24 hours.
10. If they call you from an unlisted number, no caller id.
11. If you cannot understand them in conversations.
12. If they tell you to trust them and to follow their procedures strictly.
13. If you ask for due diligence information on them and they ignore the request.
14. If you cannot verify their information.

15. If they ask for any kind of fee, transfer, insurance premium, etc.
16. If you get a very weird feeling in you stomach!

Chapter Four
FRAUD

Fraud is the premeditated deception of another person for personal gain of some kind. This category and money laundering can get us in huge legal trouble. Whether we have knowledge of the fraud or not, we can seem to be as guilty as the fraudster. It could easily get one of us, an innocent investor, in a situation where at best we have to spend a lot of money defending ourselves against being prosecuted. The people using us to commit fraud are out for big money, they do deals that get into the hundreds of thousands of dollars. They are far more sophisticated than the fee scammers. Without divulging any company or people's names, I would like to describe one situation I dealt with recently. Keep in mind I am not happy about my actions, and this cost me and my family a lot of money.

I will start by saying I keep numerous bank accounts with different banks, most with $0 to $100 balances, with a savings account at the same institution, so I am be able to move money around quickly. This helps me give wiring instructions to get funding, and I can move those funds to another account as soon as they hit my account. I was setting up one of these accounts at a local major bank. I asked for two people to be in the office while I was setting the accounts up. I wanted to ask questions and have witnesses. I told them what I had been dealing with in regards to fee scams, and asked specifically how quickly funds would be cleared so I had no chance of me losing money if I was asked to send a fee out again.

Not long after setting up this account I had closed a real estate deal and luckily moved those funds to the savings account. A few months later I got a call about one of my request for funding on LinkedIn. This was supposedly a broker out of New York. He told me he had a private lender very interested in my executive summary, and wanted to provide $10 million in funds. I told him I was interested and we negotiated interest and terms down from what he was asking to close to where I was thinking was fair. I told him I really needed more funding if possible. He asked the investor and he agreed to fund $20 million. The private lender supposedly asked for an insurance security policy, which I still to this day have never heard of anyone having or obtaining. But at the time I thought it may be possible, as I had been in the insurance business and knew that if you go to the right company, almost anything can be insured. So, I was willing to listen. He told me the premium would be a few hundred thousand dollars, and he had another smaller investor willing to loan this fee to me to get the deal closed. I would pay him back a big profit on this small loan, which made sense to me and was well worth it to get the $20 million closed with the terms I had negotiated. I was told they had to get the paperwork to the insurance company which would take two weeks, and I waited two weeks. He told me after the insurance money was paid, he and another person would come to meet me and to see some projects for due diligence, and then they would fund the loan in one wire transfer. Keep in mind this had no security with this insurance. The broker told me he would be sending three separate wires to keep the amount under $100,000 so the bank would not flag them. The first wire was sent for $110,000 to my account. He then asked me the next day to send it to some offshore account. This particular bank required me to come into the bank to wire any funds. I went in the next day, and luckily they would not wire the funds. God was again watching over me. The bank had flagged the funds for any international wire for five days, which was on a Friday. On Thursday the broker gave me some reason he wanted $5,000 wired to an account. At this time the funds were cleared and I was safe in that regard. I live a good ways away from the bank and did not have time to go in to do a wire. This deal had been going very well with no odd situations coming up and no pushing, I actually had to wait on his schedule. They gave me no reason not to believe every word I was told. This guy was very professional, kind, and his e-mails were very well put together. So, since I would have had to go to the bank, I just wired the $5,000 from another bank account at another bank which would do it over the phone. Bad idea! I was shocked at what happened the next day. I was asked to finish the wire we started on Tuesday. I went into the bank and asked the wiring person to do the wire. She got into my account and her mouth dropped, I could see her concern without a word spoken. I ask her what was going on and she said my accounts were frozen, all of them.

I assume she had a note to call the fraud department at the banks home office, because she immediately made a call and stayed on the phone for about fifteen minutes. When she was finished she told me that the funds in my account would be pulled and all my accounts would be closed. She told me a bank teller in New York had taken the funds from an imposter and placed them into an account that was not his, and then wired them to me. This was the same bank, so it was a bank to bank transfer, and not a bank wire. This is more of an internal transfer, which is different than a wire transfer. They caught the problem, and she told me it was a deposit of counterfeit cashier's checks! I had most of the money I paid my bills with in the savings account not affiliated with this checking account. They froze that account too and I had almost no money for over a week. I told her I had a good bit of information on this broker, but no one ever called me to ask any questions. About three weeks later I got a check in the mail for my balances on the accounts, but they were closed completely. After doing appraisal for this bank for thirty years, borrowing untold amounts of money, and have numerous checking accounts, the bank dropped me immediately. I was shocked and embarrassed. I live in a small town and things get around quick. I was not very happy, I felt like my bank had let me down.

The broker called me back and asked me when the funds were going to be wired or if they had been. I told him they were not going to be wired and he was probably going to jail. That was the last I heard from him. I waited on the banks fraud department to call me, and to my shock they never did. The important lesson to learn here is this: if you have a local bank, or a bank that has physical bank locations, get several bank accounts with online banks. Set up checking and savings accounts that are separate so money can be moved online instantly from your computer. These banks clear the funds before they go into your account. This way you are safe when the funds hit the account. International wires are generally only held for two to three days. This offers you another layer of protection. Always be leery of someone asking you to wire funds quickly. They may tell you the person providing the funding doesn't feel comfortable leaving funds in someone else's account for over a day, or give some other plausible excuse, but it is just a ploy to funnel funds out before getting caught. So, yes I have been scammed, and involved with fraud and counterfeiting, unfortunately more than once.

In a similar situation, I received an email l about a broker wanting to fund me for around $1 million with an insurance premium of $27,000. He was persistent about me paying it for over a month and I did what I always do, I said no and kept him hanging. At this time I had set up accounts at a new bank. This was another new bank locally, but a major institution. The first deal or two I had with them involved some bad checks for over $200,000 from Canada. I asked the bank employee to call and check the funds, she said she probably could not verify funds. I came back the next day and asked her again to please call and verify funds. She agreed and called. The funds were fraudulent. From that point until today she is scared to death each time I come in, but she is very good to me, because she knows of my character and my appraisal business.

So, this private lender finally called me again and now said he had an investor to pay the fee. It took several days to finally get a wire of $8,300. He wanted to keep the funds under the IRS radar of $10,000. I checked my account online and looked at the deposit. Next to it was a number with the labeled "IRS refund" next to it! I started to feel sick with worry. The next day I went back to the bank to talk to my favorite bank employee to ask her what it meant. She had no idea, but she picked up the phone and called the sending bank, which gave her the IRS number corresponding to this account. That was around April 15th, so I could not get through to the IRS when I tried to call. That same day I got an odd e-mail from a woman, who said she had been talking to a broker that I did not know. She told me he said that I would be the investor paying the fee for her loan. It hit me like a rock. I replied, "Please call me!" She immediately did, and we got pretty comfortable very quickly. I asked her if she did not mind, to give me the phone number for the broker she had spoke to. I have no idea why I thought it was the same guy, but for some odd reason I did. Of course the two names were different, but guess what, the phone numbers were the same. Talk about good luck and excellent timing. I give all credit to God for again watching over me.

Later the broker called me to get the funds wired and I happily told him he was not going to get those funds wired, and I would send him an e-mail. I sent him the copy of the e-mail the woman sent me, that he had sent her with my name and bank, and his other name but the same phone number. He was caught and very angry, he used numerous cuss words and called me a thief. Those funds are still in that account, waiting for the rightful owner to appear via our IRS. Luckily, I was patient and paid attention to my deposits online. I was leery of him from day one. I will reiterate: Your instincts are almost always correct.

Chapter Five

MONEY LAUNDERING AND EMPLOYMENT SCAMS

A s I said earlier, this category will get you in big trouble. It is hard to prove yourself innocent when you are giving wiring instructions for fraudulent funds to be transferred to another party. I had over $500,000 wired to my accounts from different people, and all of it was fraudulent. Scary to say the least, but I caught all of them before the money even hit my account. So, I came out unharmed, but I was lucky. Your safest policy is to stay away from anyone who wants to send a wire to you, unless they are a major known lender; or you can really verify who they are, where the funds are coming from, why they are going somewhere else, and who they are going to and where they are located. Money laundering is not the most common form of fraud in real estate, but it still happens to investors through lending. All they need is to get an account to transfer to and have a reason for you to send it to someone else, even if they say they are paying you for a service. I had this happen in an employment scam.

I had a man on a social media site send me a note about a collections job for a major international company. He had viewed my profile and thought I was capable of doing the job. The company was a major manufacturer of high-dollar pipe making equipment. He told me I would be collecting on delinquent accounts in North America. He also told me they had over $5 million in bad debt here and in Canada. He offered me $4,000 a month and 5% of what I collected. The accounts were huge. I negotiated the monthly salary to $5,000 a month. He sent me a contract from his company, and I went to their website and found a contact e-mail. I sent an e-mail with the contract to the CEO of the company with the company e-mail address. To this day have no idea how that got verified, but it did. I accepted the job, and I got my first delinquent account to collect. It was about $150,000. I called the number and did not get a response. The guy that hired me later told me the client was out of town and he would handle it. He sent me a second delinquent account that was in Canada. I phoned the guy and he answered. I politely told him who I was and that he owed $250,000 on his delinquent account. That's when I started to know that something wasn't right. He was too nice about it. I have worked in collections before, and not too many people are nice when you're calling them about not paying their bills. He told me he had an investor who was going to help him fund some of his debt for part of his business. He told me he could let me know after talking to them how much they could pay. He called me back and told me he could pay about $150,000 in the next week, but that he would not have the funds ready in time. I told him I would protect him as much as I could. Basically that I was going to hold his funds until they cleared, and would not send them to my company until I received a paid receipt which I would send him directly from that companies accounting department. I got a check in the mail from him for $216,000 the next week. I never made the deposit. I had the bank verify it, and it was not good.

I had already received several e-mails from a business social media site I use asking how my job with this company was going. They wanted to know because they had been contacted and hired as well. I immediately knew it was probably a money laundering or fraud scheme. I had several other calls. I told everyone I thought it was a scam because I could have collected $5 million in bad debt in a few months, and no company that large would hire several people and pay them that kind of money to collect that small of an amount of bad debt. My first instinct was right and had caught it before I had unknowingly become a participant in this money laundering scheme. Listen to your own mind! The people who are looking to take advantage of you know that we are usually greedy humans that are easily blinded by dollar signs.

Chapter Six
FEE SCAMS

This is the biggest issue for us as real estate investors, and the easiest trap for us to fall in to. The main reason is that the scam starts with one small, affordable fee but drags you in to pay more and more. Luckily these are easier to spot. Remember one thing: if they ask you for a fee upfront, typically they are scamming. If you walk away immediately you will save thousands of dollars and probably hundreds of hours of your time. These are the people that write poorly, cannot spell, and sometimes talk so you cannot understand them. I am over dealing with anyone I cannot understand. They are very pushy on time frames. Be patient and ask them for information to aggravate them, and they will make a mistake that clearly tells you they are trouble. Stick to the list of good real estate practices I listed earlier, and do not break from it, or you may be sorry.

There are some fee scammers who want to hit a home run and get a large one time fee; they have several approaches. These guys are smarter and offer bigger loans, and tend to go after bigger, more experienced investors. They have more technical skills than most. I was told by one scammer that he pulled my information off of a internet website that he had hacked. He had access to it like all other members, but he could not be tracked back to this website, or verified. They use all avenues of obtaining your personal information and then search and study you on social media sites. This information is used to play to your emotions and your personality. If you are asked to send a fee and it is going to another country, you should run away as fast as you can. Have the brokers e-mail address and phone number blocked. The initial decision to drop them is nearly always correct, and blocking them keeps you from being emotionally drawn back in to their lies. My partner and I have called and talked to over 2000 private lenders, and we put them in an Excel spreadsheet. There were only about a dozen of those that I knew for sure were real.

Another situation that I would not necessarily call a scam, because they get your legal signature to do this, but I think it is just as unethical as other illegal scams. In my opinion it is a legal way of using deception to fee scam legally. Business lines of credit. When I hear someone tell me they are going to give me a business line of credit, I think of a bank line of credit in my business name. But, be careful! They ask you to pay 15% on the credit they get approved in your contract with them. They also verbally tell you the credit will be 0% interest rate for up to 12 months. Now, let me explain what they really mean. What they will do is apply to major credit card companies for you to obtain business credit cards in your company name. There are several problems with this. First, we have to protect our credit rating. When they do all of these applications, they pull your personal credit rating, which shows as an inquiry on your personal credit report. Inquiries make your credit score go down and scares lenders to death. Second, how can a credit card with a monthly cash withdrawal limit of $2,500 really help a real estate investor buying property? It is such a small amount it would take ten cards to get together a down payment. Then your credit score really looks bad. But the worst part is the 0% interest is only for purchases of goods or services. The cash withdrawals are another story, there is a different interest rate and an additional fee for them. So in the end these so called business lines of credit are useless. These lines of credit will just get you into trouble.

One incident that really lasted forever. I received an e-mailed from a guy that said he could make me an unsecured loan from his personal funds for about $10 million. I really slow played this guy a bunch, and looking back I pretty much had a bad feeling about him from the beginning. After many conversations I told him I would not pay any fees, but if he had the funds he told me he had, we should be partners and buy properties together. I would use my credibility in the U.S. to loan his money at a higher yield than what he was currently asking. He agreed to Joint Venture (JV) on $100 million and come to the U.S. and talk about the lending partnership. He said he would pay the fee on the loan. After he said he paid the fee, he asked me for a $3,500 transfer fee. I still would not pay him any fees. This guy was relentless, and he drove me crazy with constant e-mails and phone calls. Then it got worse. Before I really knew if he was real or not, he told me he was going to use me as a reference. This put me in a really bad position because I do not recommend people I am not sure about. I told him I was not going to lie for him, and he started to get pushy about it. Even after I had said no, he started sending people to me anyway! Several of the people that had called me had already sent him good sized fees. I told them to be careful, that I had not received anything from him and did not have any idea if he was legitimate or not. I also told them what he had agreed to do with me. Here is the part that is important. He was still trying to get me to pay a transfer fee, as he was telling me he had a plane ticket to fly here and discuss our partnerships. I asked to see the ticket, which he sent later that day. I immediately called my partner who helps me do internet searches. I asked him to do what he could to check the flight information. In ten minutes he sent me the copy of the same ticket cancelled. All I can say is my partner did an awesome job, and I was amazed he could get that kind of information that quick.

Needless to say this guy is on my public scammers list, and I ended all correspondence with him for good. Who would have thought to buy a plane ticket and cancel it to show proof (fraudulent) so he could finish his scam? They are smart and will go to great lengths to take our money. What really bothered me were the two women who had called me after they paid their first fee to him. I did not know about him at that time, even though he was sizing up to be a pushy scammer, I really could not tell these ladies he was. He had played them to me telling me he would pay my second fee if I got them to pay theirs. This was in no way appropriate in my book. I spent a good bit of time talking to these two women, and tried my best to get them to do as much due diligence as possible, but they were already hooked by having invested in this deal already. That is the scammers hook. They get you to pay the first small fee, then in your mind you will lose the first fee if you do not pay the second one. But in reality you have already lost the first one. Don't chase good money after bad. Cut your losses, get over it, and save your money.

One week I turned stupid and decided to risk a few thousand dollars on what I would pick as my best chances of getting funded out of hundreds of lenders I was talking to at the time. Yes hundreds! The first lender was out of California. He seemed very nice and when we talked on Sunday for a minute he apologized for not getting back to me because he had been at church. This always gets me! I put faith in people that say they have God in their life. Trust me most people who bring up personal information like this are just playing you! He told me he would loan me $1 million with no security except a small fee of $750. At the time I felt fairly good about this guy and I sent the money. I did have his contract and a loan agreement in hand and completed. After receiving the $750 fee he told me there would have to be an insurance payment of about $10,000. I of course blew my top and went off on him about not disclosing this cost. This is illegal! After many angry conversations, he told me to calm down and that he was working on getting the fee paid. He said he had $6,000 of it and asked me to pay the other $4,000. Of course, he had got all he was getting out of me. This went on and on for a month or two and he kept telling me he was still working on getting the other part of the fee. He was using the time to ease the pain and anger that I felt. You know the story, he finally disappeared into nowhere.

The second guy was one of my top picks. He promised several million with only a small fee. I sent the fee and of course, he immediately sent a request with a second fee. I was so angry that I actually hunted him down, and told him I was going to pursue him and the person that received the wire. He pretty much just played games with it and had no concern as to what I might do. Several months later he e-mailed me again and tried to set up an even bigger scam. I caught it right away this time, and realized this guy was a serious player in this scamming business. He had no fear of being caught and would go to great lengths to keep his contacts on a leash.

The third person again used his religious beliefs to draw me in. He quoted scripture, many "Bless you's" and other ridiculous lies. He told me he had an attorney that would handle the transaction. This pleases me in most cases, as it gives you someone to check out and verify. They required an insurance policy for security and gave me the insurance company's name. This so called attorney was very straightforward and professional. I kept pushing to fly out to California to meet for the closing. They pushed to do the deal in a wire transfer, which was my first red flag. I then began checking on the attorney. The actual private lender was online, and the insurance company was real. But it kept giving me a weird feeling. So, I sent an e-mail verification to the insurance company. Finally after several e-mails and a phone call they told me they did not do collateral based insurance policies. To make a long story short I found out the private lender was using another wealthy person's identity, and the attorney and the private lender was the same person, playing both roles.

Take my word for it, do not think throwing out several chances to get one deal done will increase your odds of closing a loan at all. I am a bit of a risk taker at times, and this week burned me and taught me some valuable lessons. I was arguing with a professed and proud scammer one day, who told me he had taken $60,000 in one upfront fee a few days before from one person. I told him my private investigator could track him down with his IP address. He said go ahead, but then he threatened to hack my computer if I did! I think he was serious. He confessed to hacking into a major private lending website and getting my contact information. This shocked me that it could be that simple for someone in Dubai to get into a major site and steal information. Then he wanted to argue with me about how he was a Christian! I won't even touch that.

After dealing with all of these scam artists for years, I made a serious commitment to only doing big potential lending deals face to face. I had several contacts from international private lenders. I had been dealing with one in London for six months and they never quit begging me to give them a chance. I am still getting e-mails today that I ignore. I was so skeptical about this one I went well above my normal due diligence. Keep in mind I have talked to U.S. Embassy people around the world, and searched financial records for businesses in numerous countries; whatever it takes to verify information. This lender seemed to be ok, but had a few bad internet reviews. I asked for references and was given six. I contacted all of them, and they all gave very good references, which means nothing of course, but at the time seemed better than a bad online review. I went back and looked at her website closely and at the information my internet search had pulled up. She had a Financial Conduct Authority (FCA) license number and an address in London. I was looking online for due diligence information on her using this license number, and happened to catch another company with the same number and same website, with minor differences. So I called the FCA in London to ask why both companies had the same number. In the meantime, after seven months of dealing with her, I told her the only way I would do business was to meet face to face. She agreed and we started making plans. I was getting deeper and deeper into questions and answers to try to catch her in a mistake. Some odd things started popping up, and it led me into more Google searches where I found numerous complaints about her. I called the bank she provided as proof of funds, and they had no idea who she was. This was just before I was about to buy a plane ticket to meet in London. The final word came when I received an e-mail from the FCA in London telling me the other company was legitimate, and the license number she was using was theirs.

Chapter Seven
JOHANNESBURG

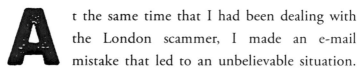

At the same time that I had been dealing with the London scammer, I made an e-mail mistake that led to an unbelievable situation. The story of my stupidest move ever will finally serve a good purpose, and give this book some true substance and clarity on how things can get really out of hand. I had been corresponding via e-mail with two David's at once. As busy as I am, I mixed up two brokers, and did not know them apart. One day I sent a note to one David that I thought was a scammer, and the other David got it. He sent me a nice note back and told me he thought I had sent it to the wrong broker. He also said that he had a private investor with a much lower rate than the deal I was discussing. Well, that got my attention. We had talked several times before, and he was in Johannesburg, South Africa. At first glance this threw up major red flags, and that is why I had dropped him off my radar for a month.

This guy got lucky and he caught me in the right mood, at the right time. I was already thinking I was going to be flying to London for a meeting with the above lender, an off-market broker I had done business with, and another lender I had been dealing with. I decided a trip to meet with three people would be worth it. But after realizing the main lender was a scammer, this African deal started to look really good. No fees upfront, and only some costs affiliated with legal work that would be paid at closing. The closing would be done with a face to face meeting at a major bank. I was told a major bank officer was helping a politician with mega bucks do this deal, and was keeping it quiet so that it was not publicly known. It sounded like the politician was taking government money and using it for his own gain. This is where I should have said the private lender is involved in immoral lending, and walked away. But I had made the quick (bad) decisions to go meet a lender.

The broker told me this investor would only do business in a face to face meeting in Johannesburg. So I quickly did an internet search about the city, its crime rates, and other demographics. To my surprise it was a nice city with very limited crime. It had lots of very nice amenities and businesses. The broker and I discussed my concerns of Africa and how this deal would go down. I was very precise about my questions and what I would and would not do. He was very reassuring about how safe it was and how nice the city was. I was still uncertain about my safety, but I was hooked on this deal and I thought I was only risking my travel funds. Even though I was nervous, I felt as long as I was careful I would be alright. I had a window open to travel but had some other obligations that made it a now or never time frame for me to go. He wanted me to come on the following Monday, and it was Tuesday. I needed to arrive on Thursday, do the two day deal, and return home. It all worked out. I found a flight and he took care of booking my room at a major American hotel.

I left at noon on Wednesday and would arrive on Thursday. I had a ominous feeling because my car battery was dead when I tried to leave for the airport in Huntsville, Alabama. I got it started and off I went to Africa. I knew how much the closing was going to cost, but for my safety I did not carry much money with me. I had already thought about the possibility that they may be setting me up, so I carried only limited travel funds. At the Atlanta airport while I was waiting to board, I noticed the entire flight was almost all American college students. I boarded and sat next to a guy that lived in South Africa. He was very nice and told me not to worry at all. Several more passengers jumped in the conversation and reassured me of the same. I started to calm down after seeing all the students and talking to the other travelers. I was convinced I would be okay if I was very observant of my surroundings and what I was doing. Even though I had not met the broker, I had a good feeling about him. I had a sense of being safe around him. But during the flight my mind considered all the things that could go horribly wrong. I got off the fifteen hour flight and took an hour cab ride to my hotel, which was very nice. The hotel staff spoke excellent English, and were professionals. I was worn out from the flight but my adrenaline was still pumping. The broker called me and said he would come meet me at the hotel that night, which was great with me. I wanted to speak with and see the person that was going to do business with me. We were talking about a $20 million deal!

I got a call from the front office that I had a visitor, I told them to check his ID and if it was correct to send him up. I answered the door and he was there with another man who he introduced as his brother. He looked scared to death of being in the room with me. I think if they had both been six-foot-six and 250 pounds each, I probably would not have opened the door. But they looked harmless to me. We had a great conversation and hit it off really good. We set up a meeting for the next day with the banker of the investor. It was set for ten o'clock the next morning. He kept telling me this was a big deal and needed to be handled confidentially. This was of some concern, but if the deal was as real as he was telling me I understood. What the broker did not know was that I was going to stick to my criteria that I go by, even if it did not meet his. I am very stubborn that way. I think if you can walk away from a $20 million deal then you are keeping your head focused on realistic things and not letting greed guide you.

That night we had talked extensively about how I did my investing and they were impressed. In the discussion I told him $20 million was a small number in regards to my portfolio, and being able to cost average a lot of good acquisitions and canceled out the occasional bad one. The next morning he told me he had spoken to the banker and the investor, and they both agreed to lend me $100 million, if I would do this as a loan in Johannesburg for the investor's tax benefit. Then we would do a JV, with him taking 20% after I had all the funds transferred. They were putting a lot of trust in me, and they wanted to meet and talk before making a firm commitment. This all fit with my idea of how a big investor should handle a deal like this. Discreetly, behind the scenes, wanting to have equity, and wanting to send someone to the U.S. after closing to check on the deals being purchased. I like dealing with people that work in a good business manner. Everything they asked for gave them credibility.

After the broker and his brother left I knew I had to have some money to keep from doing a wire transfer, so the next morning I grabbed a cab driver and explained my problem. I needed to come up with about 130,000 rand (the currency in South Africa), which only comes in increments of 100 and 200. So, I needed between 650 and 1300 bills. This was a problem. I couldn't physically get that many bills in my pocket! And doing it safely without drawing any attention to myself. I had read that the number one way to be a target of crime as a tourist was to show off a bunch of cash. Well the very nice cab driver carried me to Nedbank, First National Bank, and several others. I had numerous credit cards with large limits on them, but at this time none of my credit card companies knew I had traveled to Johannesburg. So, I had the cab driver carry me to Nelson Mandela Mall, a sprawling, very exclusive shopping area with a bank court inside. I went from bank to bank asking each to give me a cash advance. None would take my credit cards, not Chase, Citibank, Capital One, etc. My only option was to use ATM's to get as much as possible. This was an issue in itself. Some cards locked me out as soon as I inserted it. I had no idea what the PIN numbers were, and some had never been set up. So, I had to go back to the room and call every card company to tell them where I was and not to limit my access in Johannesburg. This worked great, but they still had limits. Daily and monthly withdrawal limits. This was a major problem, getting 2,500 rand was the maximum on most of the machines, and for some it was even less. You do the math with me, 130,000 rand divided by 2500 was 52 trips to ATM's with full withdrawals. I was really worried. If anyone was watching, they could see what I was doing. These ATM's were all out in the public view. Getting 2,500 rand at a time and trying to hide it in my pocket was making me extremely nervous. I had several thousand rand with me now, and I was worn out. I had not slept since I arrived, and the stress of gathering the cash had worn me out. My wife even went to our bank and took out several thousand dollars to send to me. But when she went to a money transfer place, they laughed at her when she told them the amount and location. They said it would get held for several days. Back in my hotel room, I tried to use my room safe for the money I had been able to get, and it was broken. Now I had all this money and my safe would not work. I called for a maintenance guy to fix it. When he did, it was obvious that he could easily get in to anyone's safe without any issue. This only added to my growing concerns.

The next morning the broker and his brother came to my hotel room, where we talked while waiting on a driver from the bank to pick us up. It was a long wait. The night before I had noticed a Gideon New Testament Bible in the nightstand. I took the Bible over to the table where we were sitting. I handed them the Bible and asked them what it meant to them. They were tongue tied, it was and seemed to them a loaded question. I was trying to weed out terrorists or extremists. After telling them I was not going to judge them for their answer, they both said they were Christians and were raised in church. The next morning we discussed this topic in detail for a good twenty minutes. This made me feel a lot more comfortable with them. I thought by talking about the Bible with them I might catch them in a lie, but they had seemed genuine and honest during our conversation.

I had befriended a couple of the cab drivers that worked for a company that kept two Mercedes at the hotel for guest at all times. These guys were great, and I will forever remember them and thank God for having them there. I think God placed them there just to watch out for me! I told them that morning they might want to get the tag number or even follow the car that was going to pick us up. I wanted them to feel as concerned for their safety as I was for mine. They were devout Christian men, all about helping a stranger in need. I could see the concern in their eyes about me going with a stranger instead of with them. I told them I would make the decision after seeing the driver and car that picked us up, and I might decide to let them drive me behind this car. The bank driver showed up and calmed my fears. He was a very professional looking young man that opened my door as if I were a king. I had no idea where we were going except that it was to a bank. We went to Nelson Mandela Square, a very exclusive part of Sandton, a suburb of Johannesburg. We drove up to the corporate headquarters of Nedbank, one of the biggest banks in Africa. This was a sprawling beautiful building that took up six blocks of the most prized property in South Africa. We did not go to a parking deck, we entered into a beautiful wrought-iron fenced private parking area. The driver drove straight to the front entrance, where we sat and waited on a women that took us into the building. This was not a public entry. She went to a check-in booth and gave us security cards that we had to keep on us. We entered a gated area where we were checked by a guard, then up a long stair case to the next floor, to a beautiful open atrium. We went down a long S-shaped hallway, and I was really trying to focus on where we were going and what was on the way. Each room had a different name, and they appeared to be all for private real estate closings, wealth management meetings for exclusive clients, or something similar. We went to the last door of about twenty, and entered a private room with a table and four chairs. The banker was inside waiting. He had the women that brought us in bring us what we wanted to drink. He then introduced himself and told me he wanted to give me a gift. He handed me a green Nedbank gift bag. It contained a wooden box with a business pen with a laser light and flashlight built into the end, with extra batteries in a special cutout in the wooden box. If you know anything about pen lasers without the pen, they are very expensive, and banks do not give them out to all there banking account holders.

All of this was very reassuring to say the least. I was very impressed. I knew getting into that building that way did not happen to an average person in Johannesburg. It was for the bank executives, top-tier clients and business owners. We talked to the banker and he told us that we were running a little behind on time and they would try to close that afternoon. It was Friday, and it made sense. They had me sign for a Nedbank account to move the $100 million to my name, then it would be immediately transferred that afternoon to my U.S. account. I knew that would be another issue to deal with when I got home but I didn't worry about it now. Think about it, $100 million wired into an account in the U.S. that previously had a balance of zero dollars. Talk about red flags for the banking people in the US! Well that was something I would deal with if it occurred. I signed the documents and I was told at this point that I needed to get a wire sent from my bank since I did not bring all the funds for the fee.

I knew all along I did not want to wire any money and this concerned me, but the night before I had tried to collect the money from the ATM's and was unsuccessful. Back in my hotel room, I was feeling really good about this deal, and had used the four hours between the meeting and the closing to think it over. So, I told them I would wire it, which I had my bank get it ready. Just before I was about to wire it, I decided I needed some ID beforehand. I sent a text to the broker and things changed. He acted like I had broken all our trust, but this is where I stick to my guns and do not waiver. I thought long and hard about the cost of the trip and time wasted, and still just could not allow myself to wire the funds. Time ran out on Friday and I told him all he had to do was send me his identification, which I am sure he had or the hotel would not have let him come to my room on that first day. He called me just after five and said the investor was cancelling because I was acting weird. I told him that was fine, and I would pack up and go home. After arguing like brothers, I think we both realized we had a lot at stake, and I still had seen no really bad signs of a scam. We settled down and I told him if it could be worked out I could probably have the funds by the next morning, but I wanted a face to face meeting like he had said to close. But the funds could not be transferred. This put me in a bad position, and I wasn't sure how it was going to work out.

We got off the phone thinking he was going to set up the closing and I would be bringing the cash in rand to the meeting. Well if I was even going to think about closing this deal I had to get my cab driver friend and go start the ATM process all over again in a hurry. My driver showed real concern and caring for me that you usually only see in a close friend or family member. He knew we were brothers in Christ. So, I asked him how late he was going to work and he told me boldly, "All night if you need me!" So we went to work gathering cash. This process made me nervous again because we had a lot of cash, and people could see me getting it. When I made it back to my room I had not eaten all day and I was worn out; but with all the stress, I still could not sleep.

The broker sent me a note the next morning that said the investor wanted him to pick up the money and see it before we closed to be sure that I was serious. This was way out of my comfort zone. I told him under no circumstances would I hand over cash to someone, especially a stranger, before closing. This really made him upset. He pretty much said it was not going to close, and again I calmly said that was fine and I would get a ticket and head to the airport. I got off the phone and packed, opened my laptop and booked a flight out for ten hours later that night. I headed downstairs with my cash and luggage. I told the hotel attendant I would be leaving a day early and checked out. As I was heading to the cab I got a call from a guy I had never heard of before. I could tell he was an older gentleman and introduced himself as Jim, my broker's partner. This was unexpected news, as I had never heard of him before. But I listened to what he had to say because earlier I had a sick feeling that possibly I had just walked away from $100 million that would have been life changing for me. So, I dropped my luggage in the lobby and had a seat. We commenced into a long drawn out argument that eventually made me think he was supposed to call me to try to calm me down and change my mind—which did not even get close to working. We parted words by me saying that we had two different opinions on how to do our business, and I was not changing. He was angry and said I was going to regret it, that they did business by trust. I told him that was fine but I had learned better over the years and would stick to my cautious business ways. A few minutes later I was back in the cab with my driver, and we headed to the bank to get my money changed into dollars. We had hardly made it out of the hotel parking lot when Jim called me back and said I should know that his partner, my broker, was related to the investor. It was his biggest deal ever, that he was hurt and angry, and that

I should call him before this fell to pieces. I told him I thought I could make it work with some understanding.

I called the broker and we agreed to meet at Nelson Mandela Square Mall at 2:00 p.m. to discuss our differences. At this point it is on my mind that he knows I have the cash with me. But it was Saturday at the mall, and it was very busy. I kept this in the back of my mind as we were discussing where to meet. We agreed I would go in and find a restaurant and get a table. I could tell my cab driver felt the need to protect me, so I ask him to come with me. We found a place that was really busy, and I let the broker know we were there. It was 1:45 p.m. At a little after two o'clock I sent a note asking where he was, and he said he would be there in five minutes. This goes back and forth until after 3:00 p.m., and I am starting to get tired, physically sick, stressed, and a little concerned. Fifteen minutes later I see him come in with an older man who looks a little shady, and was following a bit behind him. I waved at my broker and his follower as they walked through the restaurant, less than twenty feet from me. They walked out and turned right and did not come back. I went out after him and called him on the phone, and he said he would be right back. Ten minutes, then fifteen minutes later he never returned. We think maybe he has seen us, but is worried about who is with me. The cab driver is wearing a suit and looks like an attorney. After waiting an hour and a half for this appointment, having the broker pass by with his strange accomplice, and having this much cash on me made me really nervous. I did what I promised my wife I would do, I told the cab driver that I wanted him to take me to the airport. We went out of the building in a different direction. On the way to the airport the broker called me at about 4:00 p.m. I never answered, he sent a text and I never responded. Still unsure as to what I was walking away from, we arrived at the airport.

At this point I was worn down to nothing. I was physically, mentally, and emotionally spent. As my cab driver pulled up to the entry he asked if I wanted him to go in with me, to make sure I got the cash sorted out. I told him if I could make it to the airline entry for my flight, I would be fine. He was one of the nicest, most caring individuals that I have ever met. We were going to exchange contact information, but in all the stress of that day, I just forgot. I regret that very much. I jumped out of the cab and grabbed my bags and headed inside. I went straight to my airline check-in counter and told them about the money I had, and asked what I needed to do about it. They said I would be fine and it could be exchanged when I passed into the actual gate area, beyond the security checks. I checked my large bag at the counter, and headed directly to the security check. There was an older gentleman standing before the entry. I repeated my story and assured him I did not want to run into trouble going through the security check. It seemed to alarm him, and in another language, he called for an attendant. The man who arrived wore a white shirt, and I could tell he was a supervisor. I could barely understand him as his English was not very good. He seemed to be telling me he would help me get through the security check. As I went through the security checkpoint, he seemed to be supervising it, talking quietly to the security people at every step. I took my laptop out and all my pocket garbage and headed through the metal detector. On the other side a security guard was waiting to pat me down. As he did this he felt the cash in one of my front pockets. He asked me what it was and I pointed to the guy in the white shirt and said he is taking care of it. That seemed to be good enough and he let me though. The white-shirted man came over to me and started talking. I was trying to understand what he wanted, and finally I got it. He wanted 5000 rand for getting me through. I looked at him dumbfounded and I think he thought I was balking at the price, and not just stunned that I was being asked at all. He lowered his price to a couple thousand rand. He implied I would have a problem leaving without him helping, leaving me stuck. This was directly opposite of what Delta Airlines had just told me two minutes earlier, but there was no backing up or turning around at this point to ask them for help.

Not knowing what else to do, I agreed, and he told me that he would meet me on the other side of the customs checkpoint.

I went to the currency exchange office that was a part of the customs checkpoint, and again started telling the story of why I had all this cash. They said that with that amount of cash, I had to have a receipt to get it exchanged. Most of the cash had come from ATM machines, and I had not kept all the receipts. I started to panic, as I could only find receipts for about 15,000 rand of 40,000 rand I had. But then I remembered I had received an e-mail alert notice from my credit card company with all of the withdrawals showing. They let me e-mail them a copy of that alert, and the clerk nicely counted out my cash and swapped it over.

As soon as I walked out of that office the white-shirted man was standing there, and I knew I was stuck. He walked me to the restroom where he wanted me to go into a stall with him, and another guy who appeared to be a janitor kept watch outside. I did not waste time. I knew that he might find me, so I had kept 2000 rand that I didn't exchange just in case this happened. I reached into the stall and handed him the cash and turned around and got out of there. I felt like I had been abused, I was literally sick to my stomach and shaking. I walked the long airport hall to the next restroom to regain my composure. Luckily the rest of my wait passed without incident, and I finally on to the plane for the long ride home.

The broker sent me an e-mail the next day. I responded by telling him I was home, and would take my travel loss and leave the deal alone unless he could calm down and explain things. The banker then called me, and I ask him to verify the funds and his information. He sent me a Nedbank statement with my name on an account with $100 million in it. I asked him if he would wait while I called the bank to verify funds, and he never responded. The broker then sent me another note, and told me the funds had been removed and the deal was off. I replied asking him how they could withdraw funds if the account was in my name, but received no response. You decide what happened. I am not going to lose any more sleep over it. Hopefully my experience will show you just how crazy things can get, how cloudy and unclear things can be, and how hard it can be to know what is real and what is not.

Chapter Eight
OTHER SCAMS

IDENTITY THEFT

Identity theft is the stealing of someone's personal information for personal gain. Every time you give out or list your e-mail address, name, address, phone number, or where you work, you are potentially making it easier for someone to: tap into your computer, steal your banking information, ruin your credit, or learn the details of your personal or business life. In a short period of time they can virtually become you! Even the FBI internet site on identity theft says you cannot prevent it. But, they have a good list of loss prevention techniques.

The problem with this scam is that it sometimes does not show up for months, or you never even find out it happened. I have numerous stories to talk about in this chapter, most happening when I first starting searching for private funding.

The first one was a lender out of Atlanta. I had a contract through a Realtor of mine in Tennessee on ten resort homes in a short sale for $1million, worth about $1.8 million. These properties had a very good income stream and I was going to resell them one by one, while I was renting them on a nightly rental program. Right out of the gate this lender seemed very savvy, knew the business well, and she knew I was good at what I did. She talked big business and promised to get me involved with a big investment group she was working with. It sounded like a great deal, we would partner up on $100 million in purchases and development projects. But first she gave me a $15 million LOI at a very low rate and hardly any closing costs. Trust me, this girl was very good at what she did. She asked me if I needed capital, and of course if you are a real estate investor you can always use capital. So she had me fill out and sign an application, giving her the ability to search for credit for my company. Keep this in the back of your mind for a moment. While all this was going on, I was about to need funding to close the loan on this purchase. One night I had a guy call me and tell me he was going to try to work out the funding for this project. Of course this shocked me, and I asked him who had given him my information. He said the lender had given it to him. I asked him if he knew her or had any previous dealings with her. He said he had not, and he hardly knew her. We started talking about terms, I always ask before I spend weeks wasting my time. He explained his rate and the other details of the loan. His rates were double what I had on my LOI. His terms were okay, but not even close to what she had quoted. She had told him she could not get the funding worked out and wanted him to help me. At this point I knew I had a major problem. No funds ready, and I was already in an extension on the contract. Well it went on and on, my Realtor and I both had to apologize a lot to save our reputations on this deal. It had the bank, selling broker, and owner tied up for months. It was clear she was blowing a lot of smoke and really had no idea if she could get funding or not. Later I decided she did not intend on ever trying to work the funding out.

Not long after this happened a delivery truck pulled up in my yard. I didn't remember ordering anything, but it's pretty common to get packages, so I didn't think anything of it. But when he handed me twelve envelopes from a major credit card company I got really concerned. Even more so when I saw that three of the envelopes each had

different names. I immediately opened them. I knew if I
the cards were delivered to me they were probably in my
name and I was responsible for them. After opening each
one I found two had unlimited credit available, and the
another one had a $10,000 limit. They were in the broker's
company name so I called her. She pitched a fit when I
said she was not getting them. She said they were hers,
and we would share in the use and I was not responsible.
I didn't believe that for a second. I immediately called the
credit card company and asked them who was responsible.
Of course I was, for every card. The next time I spoke to
the broker she was very nasty, and she even threatened to
sue me. For what I couldn't imagine. I had all the cards
cancelled. Thank goodness they delivered them to me
and I had enough sense to see clearly what was going on.
Six months later I got a collection call from a credit card
company for a $4,500 charge off, a week later another call
on another $5,000 charge off which I stopped before it
showed up. I cleared them up quickly but it was a waste
my valuable time. There is no telling how many deals were
turned down because I had no idea that was on my credit
report. Now I keep a credit alert monthly and check my
credit file weekly.

One day I was at home working on an appraisal and
I got a call from a man I never heard of. He introduced
himself and told me he saw my driver's license posted on

a business social media site. He checked it out because he knew me from the site, and knew that it would have been odd for me to post my license. So he read my profile and decided to contact me to let me know. A lender had posted it saying they were me. Using my credentials and character to draw people in for a lending scam. I have no idea who it was or how they got it.

Here are a few things to do to try to avoid identity theft and fix problems if it does occur. First, do not give out personal information to anyone before doing a very thorough check on them. Then, be very slow to provide information until you have complete comfort in dealing with them. Sign up for a credit monitoring service which notifies you immediately when someone pulls credit or any activity shows up on your credit file. Check your credit file weekly to see if any new inquiries or accounts have been set up. If new accounts have been set up, inquire to that company and explain they were not authorized by you. They will almost always have to remove the account from your name and any balance. You can also check inquiries to see why they are checking your credit.

CIRCUMVENTING

This is not as rampant as up-front fee scamming. It is not something you can control very well either. What happens is relatively straight forward. Someone involved in the purchase process steals your deal or property before you can close. They can do this in several scenarios. They can act like your Realtor, off-market agent, lender, broker, etc. When you use them with confidence you usually relinquish detailed information on the property. If they think the deal is really and outstanding purchase, then they may try to make the deal fail in some way so they can obtain the property themselves. There are many things they can do depending on what role they have in your deal. For example, if they are the lender, they do not let your loan get approved. This can be done by changing material facts on the application or information on the property itself, so the actual lender will not approve your funding. Then they go back and obtain the contract on it and close with a third party as the buyer. Luckily, this is not too common. But if you're in the middle of a deal and things suddenly falling apart for no apparent reason, it's possible someone is trying to circumvent you. If you have a suspicion that this is going on, start documenting all the details and keeping checking on the property availability. If you lose the contract, see if it sells shortly after. You can locate the buyer in public records. If you can, find a connection between your contract and the buyer on the public records. If you do, you will need to hire an attorney. It will be hard to prove, but could be worth the effort if the property was an exceptional buy. I have personally not witnessed this act, but I do have a non-circumvent form I get filled out and signed if I am concerned in the slightest. These can be obtained online or from your attorney, it's always best to be prepared.

COUNTERFEITING

Counterfeiting is producing a document, currency, artwork, or other valuable item that is not the original. If you get funds from a check in the mail, you had really better get your bank to check those funds before you need them. It is much simpler and safer to ask your banker to call the source to verify the funds. If you deposit it and wait for your bank to verify them in your account, you have taken those funds. You could be accused of having had prior knowledge of the funds not being real. Forgery is a related concern. If someone gets your checks, or can produce an accurate counterfeit, they can try to replicate your signature. Keep this in mind as you do business and use checks. Be careful with your checks, written or unwritten! These are not as widely used as scams, but can be just as bad if not worse if they happen.

Chapter Nine

THE TRUTH ABOUT PRIVATE LENDERS AND WHAT THEY WANT TO FUND

The fact is that out of all the private investors you will run across, I would say less than 10% will be legitimate. One reason is the bigger real private lenders do not call you, they wait on you to call them. When dealing with private lenders, if they call or e-mail you, be suspicious of them. Start your due diligence immediately. You can do an internet search for the top ten private direct lenders and they will be real. But their lending criteria are firm and they may not be available to you. The best way to find and deal with a legitimate private lender is find a verified source and call them directly. Don't just sit back and let all the scammers engage you, this will eat up your valuable time. When you are in need of funding for a deal, sometimes you can get aggressive and lose patience. This will get you in trouble. It opens the door for scammers to engage us with their lies and deceptions. You initiate the conversation with those you want to deal with. Find a verified lender with website, check their guidelines and loan terms and conditions, and see if they are interested in the types of properties you are interested in. If it seems like a match, engage them. This will save you a lot of grief and frustration.

We have also discussed this previously, but it is worth talking about in detail. The first thing we have to do to understand the lender, is to put ourselves in their shoes. Lenders want to loan money on things they feel they might have bought if you did not have the deal already. They are looking for a knowledgeable, experienced borrower. They look at many of the same things that you look at. They want properties in good locations, with solid tenants, and sufficient income to pay the expenses and debt service. They want you to have skin in the game. They only want to loan about 65% of the ARV value. That is the value they would give if purchasing themselves. When they fund a deal, they look at the worst outcomes. They want to be sure that if you fail to pay, it will still be profitable for them. Even if you have a great deal on contract, they do not know for sure that you have the capability of managing it, or the work ethic. This is always an unknown to them. If you do not have experience that is exceptional, ask someone you know to partner with you that does have experience. There are a lot of private lenders who will fund deals. But if they are individuals and not businesses, then you must have a direct connection to them or typically they will not fund you. A private individual with the funds to lend, can easily find someone who wants to borrow their money. They are more likely to choose someone they have a direct relationship with. Why would they fund a deal for someone in that they have never met or do not know anything about? You need to be realistic. Think about these scenarios, if you were the lender which of these two scenarios would you fund?

A. An investor in your area that you know wants to buy a distressed building with a major pharmacy tenant at 70% LTV.
B. A new investor one state away wants to buy a large farm to start a game hunting resort.

Answer: A. The building in A has a discounted price and income with a good tenant.

A. An investor with twenty years of experience in rehabbing wants to buy a hotel and needs 80% financing.

B. An investor wants to buy a vacant strip mall two states away with 10% down.

Answer: Neither. The rehabber has no hotel experience, and want to borrow too much. The investor in B doesn't have enough money down and is too far away for this LTV.

A. An investor in your area with little cash, but has an approved bridge loan to pay 30% down on a vacant distressed faith-based building, because it is only selling at 50% of its cost to build back.

B. An investor with ten years of experience in the rental management business wanting to buy a distressed 85% occupied 100 unit apartment complex in a good location with 30% cash down he has in the bank.

Answer: B. Choice A has no risk to himself, he is buying based on the cost to build back, not market value. The faith-based building has only one specific use, who will use it or buy it?

This is a story about a legitimate lender that left a bad taste in my mouth. I will not name the company, but they are in the top twenty direct private lenders in the country. Let me start by explaining the deal itself. This was a property in Huntsville, Alabama, in a great location. The

City of Huntsville had spent millions on a plan to expand the entire city west to Interstate 65, almost doubling the size. The plan had one major road from I-65, and several others meeting in one location. This road junction was adjacent to my property, making it one of the most prime spots possible. The probable traffic count for this property could have went to 100,000 cars a day. It was a two story mixed use building and was still being completed. It had 14,000 square feet of retail space encompassing four large units, and a restaurant on the end with an outside seating area. The upstairs had a rear entry for ten two and three bedroom high quality apartments. One apartment and one small retail unit was only framed and still needed to be finished. The prior owner had obtained financing for the construction and they had an appraisal about a year old for $1.8 million as is. This was before the plans for the city expansion became public. The restaurant tenant wanted a liquor license to sell drinks, which was not permitted in the county. But, they had requested to be re-zoned into the City of Huntsville, which would make it legal. The owner of the property had applied and it had been re-zoned. He then lost the property to his local bank.

I am not sure if they knew at this time or not, but the City of Huntsville required them to install a complete sprinkler system, which was not disclosed or possibly even known before I came along. I had obtained a contract for $625,000 with my normal due diligence period. I had obtained an LOI for funding for $800,000 to buy and complete the construction. It had one apartment and one small retail space that needed the interior finished. I started my due diligence, and first thing I did was to call the city building inspector. He made me aware of the sprinkler system. I obtained a bid from a well known company, which came with a revised contract for $550,000. I was laughing at how cheaply I was going to get to buy the property.

We had everything worked out. The contract was complete, my due diligence was done and cleared, and the lender had approved everything. I had to pay $4000 for the appraisal upfront, and was still waiting for it to come in. They had given me a timeline for it to be completed of two to three weeks. Two weeks went by and three, then four and still no answers. After some angry phone calls from me, they gave me a verbal value of $1.2 million. This was outrageously low! I knew something was up and finally I got word that they were not going to make the loan. The first reason they gave was that someone had approved a loan above 100% of the purchase price, which they did not do. This was the first I had heard of this, as everything was made clear in the detailed loan request. Later I demanded a copy of the appraisal I had paid for.

They did not want to give it to me. I threatened to file a lawsuit, and finally I got it. The appraisal came back with a value of $475,000. I cannot begin to tell you how mad I was! I am sure someone paid off the appraiser to come in low so the lender would not get sued. I was embarrassed to be an appraiser myself at that moment. It was one of the most unethical decisions and moves I had ever seen. It cost me cash out of my pocket, time, and a huge potential profit, now totally gone. The moral of this story is: Even a good lender can go terribly wrong to save their own butt!

Chapter Ten

THE IMPORTANCE OF ESTABLISHING GOOD RELATIONSHIPS!

I f you want to survive in this industry you will soon find out it is all about relationships and connections. Creating those connections takes a lot of time, and it may seem useless at times. But when out of the blue one of those contacts decides they like a deal you have, and their value becomes obvious. Remember when I said that my partner Eric and I spent almost two years contacting potential lenders? Eric would do the cold calling to the lenders to discuss their guidelines, what property types they took, what locations they liked, and what their terms were. He kept all of this information in a spreadsheet.

This way we could go back and find a specific lender for a specific project. If we needed a lender for an office building in Tennessee with rates below 10%, we could check our spreadsheet to find one. All of these contacts were originally found on social media sites or from Google searches for private lenders. On the initial phone call he would always end the conversation by talking about me and my experience, and what we had in mind. If everything was good, he would set up a conference call for all of us. This gave me some insight about the lender before the call. I could then decided if they would be able to work with us at some point, or blacklist them.

Eric had little experience in real estate, but was very good at talking to people and organizing. We were just trying to get off the ground with some ventures together. I was trying to help him as much as possible. I had purchased a six-plex condominium building in Pigeon Forge, TN. I had stolen it! It was listed for around $500,000 and had a tax assessment of around one million. It needed some rehab, but nothing significant in cost, mainly paint and carpet. I told my Realtor I wanted to make an offer, with no clue as to where I was going to get the money to pay for it. This was a bank owned property, and they had already started vacating the units to rehab them. They had two done and four empty and the two remaining tenants were not paying. So I told my Realtor I wanted to make an offer. I wanted to offer $240,000, which she said would be way too low. I do not think she really wanted to take the time to write it up, but we were good friends and she went ahead and started the process. I ended up offering $245,000 with the bank paying $5,000 toward closing cost. Surprisingly the bank accepted the offer as is. Eric and I started soliciting lenders for this project, but the search was not going well. Until Eric mentioned it to a church acquaintance, and suddenly we had found a potential lender.

His name was DeWayne, and we hit it off very well. DeWayne has a very large mission project of his own in Uganda, and I have a non-profit church camp facility. This set up some trust, but DeWayne was all business. I described the entire purchase. I told him I needed the full purchase price and $40,000 in rehab money. He agreed to the loan amount at 12% interest, with 3% at closing and a back end fee of 3% if it sold quickly. He never asked for an appraisal, just for me to send him enough data to prove the value. We spent a good bit of time going through the numbers, rehab, cash flow, exit, etc. We got everything in order and set up the closing for the funds to be wired to the local title company which closed it all via mail. It was so simple and easy.

My wife's uncle lives in this area and I live about five hours away. He had told me he wanted to do some real estate deals with me and this was a good opportunity for both of us. So I gave him 30% to handle the general contracting for the rehab, do the landscaping, and oversee the management. It worked quite well. He got everything done in 30 days and had all rented in 45 days. Everything went forward because of one seemingly small connection, that turned into a great third-party relationship. DeWayne and I have a great relationship as friends and business partners. Spend your time building these relationships and nurturing them even if you do not see where they might be going, you never know. If you know anything about sales, you know you have to meet one hundred people, to get ten prospects to make one sale. Think of these connections in the same manner. Try to make those one hundred connections through social media, local organizations or friends and family. Treat all of them seriously and stay in contact with them, you never know what may come from the relationship.

Chapter Eleven
ACQUISITIONS

I have dealt with hundreds of buyers, some of them have had billions of dollars to spend. I do not understand their thinking at times. They will buy properties with cap rates in the 4% to 6% range, or they will buy trophy hotels with little respect to what they are getting for their money. I have spent most of my life buying and selling close to my home in the small town where I do appraisal work. Most of this business was single family residence with some commercial. I found out long ago that buying ten homes worth $100,000 each that have net income of $12,000 each per year is much more work, and riskier, than buying one building with a single tenant with a triple net lease for $1 million with an NOI of $120,000. Some investors see a risk in this that they are not comfortable with. The single tenant could go bankrupt and you would lose all your income. But the ten homes are hard to manage. You are collecting from ten different families and you are doing maintenance and repairs for them.

It is true that losing that tenant could be detrimental. So, I believe buying five of the commercial properties or more is much, much safer than fifty or more of those homes. The work involved is so much less, and the risk is low on the commercial properties. My first choice of properties are distressed properties when they are available. Triple net leased by a credit tenant. Occupancy needs to be at 50-60% or higher depending on the price. I typically want to pay around 60-70% of as is value, based on the income. I want to build equity at closing while the property makes me a clear profit after any expenses and debt service is paid. If I am buying a 60% occupied building I will pay a price that is equivalent to a 10% cap rate on it's as is income. Let me clarify this with an example.

An office building with only one tenant is only 60% occupied, it is NNN leased and has an NOI of $100,000. I would pay $1 million, if it were 90% occupied I would pay only a 12% cap which is $833,000. The reason I will pay a higher price on the lower occupancy is that it has the potential to have a 15% cap when the occupancy is stabilized at 90%, so it has a value add component. Here is the math: at 90% occupied the property would have an NOI of around $150,000. If the purchase price is $1 million, then the cap rate is 15% and it will resale at closer to $1.5M. The cap rate is NOI/Purchase Price.

I like three types of properties for myself. Keep in mind I am a do-it-yourself type of guy. I will not buy any hotels because I have no experience with them. But I would buy one if I could prove that I could buy it so cheap that I could resell it in twelve months at double my money. This is very hard to prove though. I will typically not buy apartment complexes, because there are too many moving parts and you are responsible for management, employees, repairs and maintenance, grounds keeping, taxes, insurance, etc. So they are very time consuming. I wonder how many great deals I have missed while keeping up with apartments. I will not typically buy any properties with home owner's association fees, as they eat up too much of the income. I do not typically buy storage facilities, because like apartments, they take too much time and management. They are more like buying a business and not commercial rental property. I will not typically buy mobile home parks or bulk single family home packages, as they too take too much time to manage.

The types of properties I like are industrial buildings or warehouses, office buildings including medical, and retail strip centers. These are easily managed with only few tenants for the amount of income they produce. I like the warehouses and large single tenant office buildings best because I am dealing with one large tenant that you have a good idea how they pay and it is easier to find out how their business is doing because they are publicly traded companies.

I like triple net leases which mean they pay everything, all maintenance, all repairs, all taxes and insurance. I can buy and live a thousand miles away and when I close I just give them an address and I collect rent.

I want the properties in locations that are appreciating! Location, location, location. I want the leases to have at least five years unless there are no vacant competing properties in the area, and there is demand in this same area. These two things give me proof I can rent the building to some other tenant within a very reasonable time frame.

I want to buy properties I can obtain a minimum of a 10% cap rate immediately at closing, or a 12% or higher cap rate within 12 months, with increased rents or higher occupancy. I want properties in good condition without major rehab, unless I am buying considering the cost of that rehab, and I can make money off of it. This means I am buying at a price that meets my criteria plus profit after adding the rehab cost. So when I get done with repairs I add the purchase price, rehab and interest during rehab, then I can get a 13% cap rate. In this case I have made 1% higher on the cap rate, which actually means I have increased my income by 1/12 or 9.2%, 13-12=1, 1/12% cap is 9.2% added to income as a percentage. I get the property I want and for my time I may have made an extra 9.2% on the income stream for as long as the leases stay in place.

These are the criteria I look for, and are top of the line requests. Getting them all in a package at my price and cap rate is lucky and takes a lot of work. It is possible in this economy, but do not expect it.

For every purchase you make of $1 million at a 12% cap rate with a NNN lease you will make $120,000 a year less $79,836 in debt service at 7% interest and a thirty year amortization. This leaves you with $40,164 yearly in income x 10 properties is $401,640 in yearly income. This can also be done with one $10 million property. Did you notice I did not show a down payment? This is clear profit with zero down or borrowed down payment. Not bad for no money! I am not saying you can do this type of deal with no money, but if you have experience, and can buy really cheap, you may get it done with someone referring a direct private individual. Or you may have to give some of your ownership and income. Let's say the lender wants the 7% and a 20% ownership. You still make about $320,000 yearly per $10 million purchased.

Chapter Twelve
OFF-MARKET REAL ESTATE

T his is a subject not many people understand, that I felt worthwhile to include in this book. Most real estate for sale is listed with a real estate broker that has an agreement to publicly market the property via the Internet, Multiple Listing Service, newspapers, and other typical marketing sites. Off-market real estate is an entirely different animal. These are different types of property owners that do not want it publicly known that their property is for sale. There are several reasons for this. They do not want to hurt their business income by having a negative aura hanging over it, they think maybe they will get a buyer easier, and sometimes they just do not want anyone in their business. This market is typically used for commercial properties or bulk single family residences. The buyers are from several categories: Hedge funds are one of the biggest, real estate investment trusts, large family trusts, and private investors like you and I with limited funding to almost unlimited funds. Many of these buyers are international private investors.

This market is good to understand because it tells you who your competition is and how much money is in their hands, so you know to find a niche price range all these buyers stay out of. One of the best experiences I have had was dealing in off-market real estate. I still have my hand in it today. About three years ago a young man from New York was dabbling in this market and was good at talking to big buyers and sellers. He had one problem, he actually knew nothing significant about real estate. To play in this league, you need to have a long history and solid understanding of real estate. These are some of the biggest buyers in the world, the owners of the biggest and most expensive properties in the world. Do you think these people would give a normal realtor the time of day? Not on your life. They don't trust anybody. They are very smart and very business savvy.

This young man saw my profile on LinkedIn and called me for help. He was a smart guy, but at first he wanted it all, and wanted me to do all the work. Instead we negotiated an equitable split for me to help him. This meant I would find properties, and match those property characteristics to these big buyers. Honestly there are not many people who can do this nationwide and internationally to suit this clientele. I started working and within a few months I had built a very sizeable business, one of the biggest sourcing businesses around. It was very time consuming. You are dealing with buyers, sellers, and agents from all over the world, which means they call and e-mail you 24 hours a day. And when you are dealing in hundreds of millions of dollars per deal, you work when these buyers and sellers need you. Being in this market at this level gives you all the inside information about all the buyers and sellers. It also puts all the off-market inventory in your hands before even the large hedge funds and Real Estate Investment Trust's (REIT's) see the properties. They actually get them from people like myself who are working this industry.

I completely understand why the sellers use this industry to market their properties quietly. It protects their businesses from negativity in the marketplace. For buyers, I only see one positive about buying in this market. There is a lack of bidding wars. Some buyers think this is the only arena to find good deals, I totally disagree. From my experience, finding a good deal is not about where you look. It is about looking everywhere. It is about getting the entire story behind the reason the seller is selling. It is about patience and sticking to your buying criteria or guidelines, and not getting emotionally tied to any certain property. Sometimes we get tunnel vision when we find that one property we want. So much so that we give more than we typically would out of fear of another buyer coming along. This is a natural response to finding a terrific deal. Think about finding your perfect mate, we want to just go all in and lock up the deal. But in reality we need time to learn about the other person and their personality traits. Buying property is very similar, if you are in a hurry you will make mistakes, pay too much, or miss a major problem you should have found. I think by this point in the book you have heard me say something about patience twenty times or more. It is that important in buying, selling, dealing with scammers, or finding a lender. Take your time and it will save you many headaches.

Chapter Thirteen
FIGHTING BACK!

would like to talk about joining together as ethical real estate investors. We need to be proactive against the scammers and help each other out. One easy step we can take is to swap information when we see one of our colleagues being contacted on a social media site by a known scammer. We know how important time is with these people, and the seconds you take to send a warning message can make a big difference. Find a social media site or two and look for groups that post information about known scammers. Join in, and read and list any bad lenders that you have had dealings with. Be sure to only post those you are sure are scammers, we must not judge unless we have proof. I try to tell a short story of how they work so other people will be able to understand it. If someone lists a private lender as a scammer, then put them on your list of scammers. We should all have a list! Keep up with it on a spreadsheet. Include phone numbers, e-mail addresses, and any other helpful information. This way if they change their name you will still catch it with the other data. I have even caught an old scammer by having an eerie feeling that I had heard their voice before, and I was right. They had changed their name and contacted me again. Keep your guard up and go back and read the highlights of this book every once and a while as a refresher course on what to look out for. If you discover new scams or new ways they can deceive us out of our money, identity, or private information, please share that information on social media or through any means available to you. Contact me if you need help spreading the word.

It is my wish as the author and as a caring human being to help as many people with this book as possible. My hope is that thousands of people will buy the book before they get engaged with some unfortunate scam or fraud. If this book is read by private investors or anyone searching for funding from private sources, it can help save you thousands of dollars and even more in valuable time saved. I don't think it would be outrageous to say that it could save someone's life or marriage. I know that sounds bold, but if you have not been involved with these kind of people you just would not understand. To be blunt and honest, looking back over all my experiences, my impatience and greed are the only reasons I have ever dealt with these guys. I know now if I had focused on being patient and working contacts that were solid business relationships, I would have been much better off. Take my advice, and just work your local contacts and your social media contacts to build strong business relationships, and you will find real private lenders from a direct contact you know and trust. I am stockpiling many of those, which I know for sure will mean millions of dollars down the road. I wish you all the best of luck, and I am always here to help a fellow investor. Thank you so much for reading and helping my non-profit with your purchase.

FOR MORE INFORMATION:

DODD-FRANK CONSUMER PROTECTION ACT

www.gpo.gov/fdsys/pkg/PLAW-111publ203/html/PLAW-
111publ203.htm

en.wikipedia.org/wiki/Dodd%E2%80%93Frank_Wall_
Street_Reform_and_Consumer_Protection_Act

FINANCIAL CONDUCT AUTHORITY

www.fca.org.uk

UK BRIBERY ACT

www.legislation.gov.uk/ukpga/2010/23/contents

FOREIGN CORRUPT PRACTICES ACT (FCPA)

www.justice.gov/criminal-fraud/foreign-corrupt-
practices-act

FEDERAL GOVERNMENT INFORMATION ON SCAMS AND FRAUD:

www.usa.gov/topics/consumer/scams-fraud.shtml

www.usa.gov/Citizen/Topics/Internet-Fraud.shtml

www.fbi.gov/scams-safety/fraud

ABOUT THE AUTHOR

Randy Hinkle has over thirty years of experience being self-employed in the real estate industry. As the owner and manager of his own real estate brokerage, his own construction company, and as the owner of his appraisal company, Freeman Appraisal Co. LLC, he has a wealth of experience in all aspects of the real estate market. Over the course of his career, he has been involved with hundreds of construction projects, real estate investments, acquisitions, and sales. He has purchased properties from Ohio to Florida, of many different types and value ranges including condo complexes, resort properties, offices, SFR, and retail. His vision to see the end result of a project before ever starting, and working hands on with investors and builders, has made him a success, allowing him to have dealt with some of the largest buyers and sellers in the world.

He is a licensed real estate appraiser and agent in the state of Alabama, where he currently lives. In an effort to give back to his community, he founded the Stoney Creek Outreach, which has become one of the largest Christian youth facilities in the Southeast.

CPSIA information can be obtained at www.ICGtesting.com
Printed in the USA
LVOW11s2346100616

492107LV00002BA/3/P